For Terry

So great to see you. Let's keep in touch

KevinArnold@UWalumni.com
650 269 7550

10-ten

Do Not Think Badly of Me

Kevin Arnold

Manzanita Writers Press

Do Not Think Badly of Me

Manzanita Writers Press
PO Box 215, San Andreas, CA 95249
manzapress.com

Author contact: www.kevinauthor.com

ISBN 978-0-9986910-8-4
Library of Congress Serial Number: 2021925226

Cover art: *Misty Evening III* - Rachel Elise Mallon
Book Layout: Joyce Dedini-Runnells
Editing: Kathie Isaac-Luke

Dedication

Oh, to the women in my life, starting with my mother, who brought six pregnancies to term, but lost three of her children shortly after birth.

And to those who have loved me since—*three even married me. Imagine.*

Contents

Contents

Contents

Photography

You Must Not Think Badly of Me

—for Auguste and Karl Deter

We remember little of Auguste Deter,
who, in her late forties, would drag sheets
across her house and scream for hours
in the middle of the night.

She was the first woman recorded to have
debilitating memory lapses
due to a strange plaque in her brain.

Nor do we share memories of her care-partner,
Her husband Karl, a railway worker who gave up
and sent her, in 1901, to "The Castle of Insanity"
in Frankfurt, Germany.

The one we remember is the doctor
she met there, who asked,
"Where are you right now?"
and recorded her reply:
"Here and everywhere, here and now,
you must not think badly of me."

On her death, he examined her brain.
Using a new chemical, he discovered
twisted fibers—nerve tangles.
We remember Alois Alzheimer.

The Move to Memory Care

Carol had said many times,
if she got Alzheimer's, when
it's time, put her out on a farm
like her parents, who both
died of the disease.

The people from the facility and I
had set everything up. As agreed,
I'd told Carol she was going to lunch.
With my daughter Amelia,
I drove an hour from the Bay Area.

On the way down, Carol asked her,
seven times, how she was doing.
In the back seat with her,
Amelia, bless her,
found new answers every time.

Set in the middle of an apple orchard,
The facility was bucolic.
We'd set up her room with a new bed
and TV and family
and horse pictures on the walls.

They'd even put her name on the door,
which confused her. She turned to me.
I told her it would be okay.
Attendants shooed my daughter and me
away, and guided Carol to her lunch.

The Milkshake Guy

Familiar with my wife's frailness,
he almost lifts her from the car,
seats us in his busy luncheonette,
and asks if we want the usual—milkshakes.

Often chocolate, always with a cherry,
but this day I offer alternatives.
When she hears "strawberry"
she nods and smiles.

He serves us and all too soon helps her
out of her chair. With the milkshake
guy on one side and me on the other,
she bravely hobbles back to the car.

I probably shouldn't call him
the milkshake guy—he's more than that.
He's big, six-foot-three, two hundred pounds,
with a halting, smiling kindness to him.

How can I thank him for the reprieve
he's granted us: A few minutes away
from the care home down the street,
a few last moments on a date.

Invitation to the Opera

I can never toss opera invitations.
When one comes, along with the bills, fundraising
letters from my daughter's pricey college,
small magazines that published my work, journals
I keep renewing but seldom find time to read,
and those gold-embossed credit-card offerings to my ex-wife,
it's the opera offers I can't throw away.

It would be so good for the kids if I could get them to go.
Perhaps I can entice them with a familiar name—
La Traviata, Madame Butterfly, Aida, or *Carmen.*
Or maybe these colorful ads for the newer ones:
The Death of Klinghoffer or *Nixon in China*—

any program that puts the tenors in tails, the
sopranos in satin. Maybe next season, one
Wednesday, Friday, or Saturday, we'll be there
in a plush velvet seat, waiting for the lights to dim.
Imagine us in that heart-stopping quiet
just before the songs echo into the night.

Early Morning, Amherst

Soon after I set foot in
Emily Dickinson's Garden
a sleepy armed guard appears
"I've been watching" he says
"You've been careful but
underneath there are bulbs—"

We make adjustments as I wait
for my daughter to give her command
when she's ready to snap the shutter.

She wants to master the limitations of this
large-format camera her college loaned her.
It loves light and stillness, she says,
capturing motion with the sun low
is the worst use of its gift
but if you jolt the flower
at just the right moment, Dad,
we might capture
a water-droplet in mid-air.

I wait silently as, arms folded,
the garden guard watches us,
Johnna's face is hidden by a black cloth
over her head and camera. I say,
"One false move and we're dead meat."
She says "Hush," and finally,
"Now! Hit it now!"

Summer's Last Swim Meet

The six-and-unders sit in numbered chairs,
then hold hands in a daisy chain
to walk to the proper lane with their team coach
and stand nervously until the horn sounds,
when they get to splash in and make arm-windmills.
I, the false-start judge, see it all—
their legs that don't contribute much,
and the way they brush the lane markers
and breathe too often so it seems to take forever.
Still they all finish and how they beam as they climb out!
As the seven-eights take their places at the start
and at the horn dive straighter out,
stroke with more authority.

My Scotty-boy, normally no star, cuts five seconds off his best time.
As they swim, they don't breathe—coach says, after today
you'll have all fall to breathe.
The nine-tens don't hold hands but walk out knowing
this is the combined meet—all the teams are here.
Sure-footed Kate slips in her starting dive and never recovers,
trying to keep up with the eleven-twelves, who really clip along.
But it's the thirteen-and-overs who take your breath away.
They seem to cover the pool in five strokes,
their parents who've shuttled them for years
beaming over this transition from summer to fall,
childhood to adulthood—
this communal concentration on a good start.

The seven-eights take their places at the start
and at the horn dive straighter out,
stroke with more authority.

A Wave Starts as a Swell

Or the start of a swell,
or the start of a start of a swell,
then grows as our love did, until—
well, what a wave does is confront
the remains of prior waves
planes over leftovers until it suddenly crashes,
sometimes with a deadening thunder,
that moment painters paint.

Waves don't die but continue diminished,
duck under earlier waves until they
lap up on a rocky shore or a beach,
finally settle under new waves,
join a powerful undertow
—remember how we'd warn the kids?

They Are Sure I Was Never Young

"Just listen through to the third song,"
I say, when the kids realize
I've slipped my Judy Collins CD
between Save Ferris and Shania Twain.

I keep the kids' hands
from the car's CD player
while Judy sings about a time
gone by, yet, since their Mom
has moved to another town
with another man, a time still here.

After the second verse,
They chide me about Judy's
tastefully naked pictures on the jewel case,
and tell me of all my geezer favorites
—James Taylor, Bonnie Raitt, Willie Nelson—
Judy, whose photos reveal a body that
even then wasn't seventeen—
Judy's the worst.

I make them listen to her third verse,
about the possibility of a turnaround,
a happy ending. When the song ends
we drive on in total silence.

Judy Collins with Kevin Arnold at an event at Yoshi's of Oakland.
Arnold Family collection.

Umbrellas

We always want rain around here,
especially with empty reservoirs.
But the forests are wary this year.
They normally love rain, but
terrible fires have left the land
unstable, inviting mudslides.

The horses I feed have a roof
over a corner of their corral,
so they get cold
but not wet,
unless a storm blows in sideways.

One winter long ago in Madison,
my college girlfriend, who became
my first wife, came from studying
in the stacks and said she'd struck
a man with her rolled-up umbrella
because she'd looked down on the
floor of her carrel to see a mirror,
which he was using to look up her skirt.
She'd chased him until he stopped.
When he stood silent, she pummeled
him with her bumbershoot.

The corral's roof has a small overhang
which gives me a little protection
as I feed them carrots and cookies,
and I have a hat and an umbrella
and a rain jacket with a pull-up cowl
like a hoodie. It's late October and I am
oh so ready. Come, gentle rain.

First Wife

That summer before we separated
I talked her into tennis lessons—
forehands, backhands, volleys.

I would compliment her strokes
and call lines in her favor,
the kindest opponent in the world.

Afterward I hit balls to her, gentle, soft
shots that lured her slowly to the net, when
with sudden firmness, I hit the ball past her.

Japanese Graveyard on Kauai

One afternoon I drove my daughter way past Kappa,
deep into desolate cane-hauling roads.
We came upon an old graveyard on a hill near the ocean.
Before the tall cane it had overlooked the Pacific.

I got out, trying to convey my wonder to my young daughter.
The wooden markers, in Japanese with a little English,
marked the lives of turn-of-the-century fishing families.
I coaxed her out of the car and we walked

to one grave, then another.
One had fresh flowers, but most were overgrown.
I told her about once-prosperous fishing fleets,
gone now. She stood silent.

This is all that's left,
I told her at one family's grave,
after the tortuous trip from Japan,
after building the fishing fleet,

after extracting an honest living from the sea,
after constructing villages—
they're tourist towns today, I said.
No words from her as we returned to the car.

I said I hoped we had more left than that
even though I'd moved away from her mother
and watched her so silent, next to me
in the rental car dwarfed by the sugar cane.

I kept looking over at my small passenger who
wore a cotton skirt over her bathing suit,
peeking up at her father out at the edge of somewhere.
Her eyes said what can he teach me but chaos?

20

The Propeller of Everything

In my dream my son had met this girl, I saw them touching,
so I had to tell him everything at once:
the times you do it when you shouldn't,
the times you don't do it when you should;
the shame when you show desire only to have her tell you,
in no uncertain terms, that you are acting inappropriately,
the hard-walled loneliness of that;
the times when sex and love lay upon one another
not just as concentric circles but as the same circle exactly,
the times they aren't even in the same room together,
can't even shout through walls at one another,
yet sex still shouts;

how sex shadows every human interaction,
even between a child like himself and his teachers,
his mother, even his father, me; the way
sex has colored his thinking as long as he can remember,
how sex separated his mother from me,
how it's brought him to wear his bathing suit in the bathtub;
the way the women know they have it to give, or is that wrong,
do we just keep imploring them, or is all that changing;
the way those questions rattle around in the houses of our beings;
how if you include same-sex love there is no end to it,
sex propels everything; even my solitary blind mother,
his grandmother in the nursing home, is shaped by it;
the road he is about to start down has no exit—
but I wake up then, realize my son is only eleven,
I won't say these things to him now, nor probably ever—
to say things like this in real life it is always too early or too late.

Across the Decades

I'm in a theater bar on a rainy evening in Manhattan
with my son, a composer who lives nearby. We sit
in a booth discussing whether or not passion must drive
the arc of a story, how plays and novels might demand
a through story. When he gets up, guys move toward him.

Although he doesn't drink much liquor, he's obviously
among friends here. I stop following his lanky frame,
sip my Merlot and eat a breadstick. When I look up
I see him signaling to the guys to cool it. He's not
looking my way, but I can see him motion toward me.

The people coming from outside enter drenched.
We seldom have such violent rain in California.
It's been ten years since he came out to me, and
decades since I asked his nursery school teachers
if he might already be in a club I could never join.

Corduroy

If our feminist friends knew
you pack my bags, Bo,
well, we won't tell them
how you always include
lotions and pajamas

or for this trip to Seattle,
warm pants and jacket,
wide-wale corduroy,
thick peasant cloth,

so after potato salad and beer,
when I leave the bookstore,
wander down to the ferries,
the wind tries to nip at us
but it can't.

Softball in a Poetry Week

—For Galway Kinnell
(February 1, 1927 – October 28, 2014)

I

Hiking in the mountains above Squaw Valley
in the middle of a poetry week,
I had no reason to worry about anything,
but my mind was in the valley.

I'd said something stupid in the workshop that morning.
I said that more people seem to write poetry than read it.
Along the trail, when I remembered the way Galway reacted,
with a wince, I suddenly shouted "No!"

The word was loud enough for others to hear, but it
was overlooked because someone else had just remarked
how the trees change with the altitude, and how flowers
that have lost petals are still beautiful.

The "no" blurted from nowhere was my father's voice,
low, helpless, and hopeless. I looked around,
relieved no one had noticed my outburst.
I exhaled and hiked with renewed energy.

II

I was curious about what made this Galway tick.
One of the country's best-loved poets, regularly
published in *The New Yorker*—what brings him
across the country to lead this workshop?

We couldn't work on any poems we brought with us.
Every day he insisted we write new poems, and he joined
in, writing and sharing new poems daily. I loved it.
Why had I said that stupid thing in class?

III

Late in the week the poets played softball on a grass field near
Lake Tahoe. I suspected Galway, a tennis player who told us
he had played at least once on every tennis court in Manhattan,
organized the game to show his true self. He played third base,
the captain of the other team. In my first at-bat, I kept
looking at him down the left-field line and struck out.
But my second time at the plate, I managed to connect.
I hit a ball solidly, past the infield and rounded first base.

At second, short of breath, I decided to run for third.
The outfielder threw the ball to Galway, who caught it
in plenty of time to tag me out. But our workshop leader
turned the wrong way, away from me, didn't make the play.

He yelled "Safe," loudly. This was something my father
had never done for me, or anyone I could think of. This
complex, generous man had given me an astounding gift.
I started to relax, a runner at third base now.

At home plate, a Modesto poet was taking practice swings,
choking up on the bat and swinging fiercely, like this was
her one chance to pound the hell out of something.
I stood close to Galway now, his approval allowing me to

take everything in—the outfield still green this time of year;
how the pitcher set before she hurled toward the plate; the
clouds; everything. I knew now why he'd come all this way.
Galway could teach us things we could learn from no one else.

25

Long Before Separation, Squaw Valley

Can't do it tonight
no poems come.
Cannot bring pleasure,
except to my wife at three a.m. when
we throw tired bodies at one another.
At that ecstatic time my soul
makes a dying-animal sound
for how lucky I am
to be here with her.

American Shakespeare

We watch the stars slowly begin their twinkling
at Red Rocks or Aspen or a park in New York City
or a smaller town where perhaps the Rec Committee
has bent a few rules and the oft-broke Arts Commission

found some funds to get the thespians to memorize
those long soliloquies for almost nothing.
Volunteers have parked cars and ushered
people to their seats to keep ticket prices down,

so the house is packed and the meadows blanketed.
Once the players start, the amazing turns of phrase
transfix us as night moves toward total darkness
and the actors seem so close we can touch them.

In the newfound intimacy we swoon at the lovers'
kisses and that their five-century-old bawdy badinage
is still alive today. Many of us still hope-against-hope
for the lovers to make things work until we slowly admit

again what we've known along: they are star-crossed.
Still we smile as the curtain call looms, knowing Shakespeare
will proclaim an elegant order behind tonight's tragedy,
and, when the players bow deeply, we will rise.

The Colors of Jasper Ridge

You can find occasional dabs of red
or bright yellow, often a wildflower.
In August or September, perhaps
a pink Naked Lady, a Belladonna.

And you can search out some blue,
although you won't find a shade
that can compete with the sky.
Which, today, gets darker overhead.

There's brown soil and bark, and
sand by the lake and on the trails,
but no color on the preserve
can compare with the greens.

On far horizons or next to the trail,
evergreens don't seem to change.
In the fall, the green oaks may turn
vivid red surrounded by verdant grass.

Perhaps you'll see a white serviceberry
near a yellowish-green box elder or
blueish-green chaparral backgrounding
a black and orange butterfly on wing.

Jasper Ridge Biological Preserve, Stanford.

Photograph by Anthony D. Barnosky, Executive Director.

Used with permission.

Ants

Nature ain't all flora and fauna—it can
be most messy—think of rats with fleas
or the spider who bit me Tuesday night
leaving an angry red spot on my thigh.

And the ants don't stop. Yesterday
they got into the dishwasher—
I closed it and ran it on Quick Rinse,
yet two of them made it through.

Intriguing little devils, ants. First
lone scouts and later commuter lanes
They smell with their antennae
and have many ways to communicate.

Ants can kill the Buddhist in you
—Reverence for all living things—
Today they're into the recycling bin.
Should I grab the vacuum cleaner, fire it up?

The Possibility of Poise

Who could watch a squirrel—
climbing a tree or simply
bounding along the ground—
and not envy its equilibrium?

It's not that I've lived continually
off-kilter. Occasionally, in short
bursts, I've been centered, but
most of the time I've lurched.

A squirrel can even climb
a branch upside down, and that
tail will find a way to provide
whatever's needed for balance.

Imagine how collected I might be
if, every time I lurched right,
some marvel would provide
a counterweight on my left?

Aerobatics in Time of War

I had to rise at oh-dark-thirty,
throw on a one-piece bright-orange flight suit,
listen carefully to the flight instructors,
salute almost everyone,

and finally don my aviator
sunglasses and go up alone,
take a nimble aircraft aloft
for the fun stuff, the aerobatics,

where I could do things like a "stall,"
intentionally pull the nose straight up until
the wings lost their lift and my two-ton aircraft
would free-fall almost silently, thousands of feet.

I fought my instincts and relaxed in the slow spiral
until I felt some push-back from the stick,
then pulled with all my strength, both hands, and braced
for the 4-G jolt as the wings regained their lift

and I could level out, much closer to earth now.
Those puffy cumulonimbus clouds that formed
along the Florida gulf against the blue water
seemed more vivid as I regained control.

I found myself shouting my secret mantra:
I will not go to Vietnam.
I will not go
to Vietnam.

Kevin Arnold, Valletta, Malta, 1969.
Arnold Family collection.

Monterey Bay with Whales

On a bright day, I'm overlooking
the magnificent Monterey Bay again.
I mimic the way the Navy taught me
to scan the horizon many years ago.

You don't really scan. You look in one
direction, long enough to focus, before
you move your gaze twenty degrees,
pause, then focus again and again

until you've examined the entire vista.
Today no sea otters but a leaning sailboat
near the Santa Cruz harbor and a freighter
way out on the horizon, a mere dot.

My scanning is interrupted by a pod
of two or three whales not far from shore.
It's springtime, so they've come from Mexico,
where they've been breeding, heading for

the arctic, where they'll feed with their calves.
I spot pods of whales or dolphins on almost
half of my visits to Monterey Bay. Unlike
dolphins, who skim the surface, when whales

dive, it can be five or ten minutes before they
reappear. Eventually, nearby, the pod resurfaces.
One of them, probably the mother, spouts lustily—
an outpouring well worth the wait.

Coming Home Late in a Marriage

Nose around the small costly house.
You open all the shutters, I'll open all the doors.
Has the neighbor girl kept the dogs fed?
Look, on the patio—at least they have water.

I'll sort quickly through the mail.
Oh I think we're overdrawn, that check didn't clear.
Granta says they're seriously considering a story.
And three rejection slips—two for me, one for you.

Bigger and Terrier are looking old, is that heat rash?
Never thought I'd miss the dogs so.
Puppy Molly has grown again,
I felt bad leaving her, so young.

I'll go out for milk.
What else do the kids need to get through tomorrow?
How does it feel being back?
Is there beer?

Any word from Mom or her nursing home?
Check the answering machine—
the Visa-lady only gave us till the twenty-fifth.
Chit-chat nervous as a couple before a funeral.

Returning

You can't go home again but

just once you have to go back.
Must call time out—yell "t. o."
Say, life you have beaten me—
Mom, I need to come home.

After shelter and soup the ghosts return.
Your weariness, compared to your parents', is fresh.
         What can they do but feed you?
                 —Mom cooked lambchops we couldn't afford.
                 Soon, back in the world,
                 not long after, hungry again—
                 this *going-forth* we all try to avoid.

Norfolk Island Pine

If you study the pine in my front yard, you'll see
it must have gotten almost no sunlight early on.
Its early branches, down low now, were stubby,
misshapen with only slight hints of green,

but somehow this tree made it through those
early years, still pitiful at four feet, then six
feet, where it seems to have caught some sun.
At seven feet, finally, the branches start to look

the way a Norfolk Island Pine is supposed
to look. The taller branches are fuller
yet, but if it weren't for those perfectly
shaped top deep green branches that

reach eagerly for the sky, that seem to look
exactly the way a Norfolk Island Pine was
supposed to, I never would have seen myself
in the tree. A strong finish after a tough start.

If you were adequately nurtured as a child,
if your mother wasn't addicted to pills and your
dad could hold a job, you probably just see
a tree with a heartier shade of green on top

than one would expect. I'm most thankful
to those teachers who taught me to stand up
straight. Some of them even lifted me on
their shoulders to help me find my own sun.

My Parents Before Me

A photograph of them
courting in Charleston,
the Dartmouth man
sent south by GE,
a dark suit with
a touch of handkerchief.

Her gloves held in her left hand,
she looks unfettered, far from
her mother on the farm
downing pills by the handful.

Her curve hugging beads
caught in mid-sway
give no hint she will follow
in her mother's footsteps
her care will become his life—
just this snappy couple
stepping out.

John Bailey Arnold and Carolyn Ayres Arnold.
Arnold Family collection

Separation

There was no Saxon word for separation,
for the sun rising on my family
in one place and me in another.

Saxons used words like broken or torn.
I wander aimlessly to the library,
open this magazine, that book.

Before Sylvia Plath put her head in the oven
she taped the doors to her children's rooms
and made them snacks for when they awoke.

No one seems to know why Ted left her,
his wife who was giving sixteen hours a day
to the little family they had formed together,
but was, before she put her head in the oven,
slightly broken, more than a little torn.

On a hunch, I confirm there was
no Saxon word for suicide, either.

Divorce Albums

Next to the wedding books, they
hold a packet for lingerie from secret dates,
with disintegration chapters
for Christmas cards not sent,
children's lunches unprepared.
A place for the counselor and lawyer bills
real estate commission statements
and photographs of the couple in various stages
of exhaustion, longing, even hatred. An entire section
is set aside for the day the kids are told
the two who brought them forth are irreconcilable.

Leather-bound, gold-stamped books are provided
for those who reconcile, wide publicity for
the smiling faces of those who beat the odds.
And the others always have their
wedding and divorce books side by side.
The wedding may have been for the parents,
but the second album is theirs alone.

Like Air

I will never forget the moment I first believed
I was born in God, part of a plan so intricate
no mortal could possibly understand it.
That Friday I forgave Billy for tripping
me in the bushes and kicking me—
all was forgiven that day. I was on the path,
and with each breath I let God

        hold me

the way I'd held that stuffed animal, that limp lamb
I clung to after my dog Maverick had been hit by a car.
After Maverick died, his head on my knee, I held the lamb
and started yelling at my mother about Billy—why
couldn't she have been there and told Billy I'd been sick,
that I'd been in a coma, near death? Yet that Friday I knew

        no one ever dies.

God would forgive me for yelling at my mother,
and I knew, after Billy was punished, he'd be forgiven too.
Forgiveness would be everywhere, like air. Maverick
was in heaven or on his way. All things happen at once,
and the joy I found as a child is still part of me today
(though it can fade so easily). Joy can be, should be,
ours right now. And it can be for ever. You know, forever.

Hooky from High School

Mom's out of Elgin hospital
helping me play hooky

she buys me a mint-chocolate
milkshake and takes my hand

her face is so much more calm
after these dryings-out

her eyes follow my every word
as if I were a poet

Yesterday among Friends

In the cool evenings of this altitude,
when I go out on the deck
at the tail end of a divorce,
the mountains seem to know
nothing's turned out as I planned.

Yesterday I broke down when a poet revealed
what she had to do to escape her own father.
Pain in other people's lives seems unbearable.
The pain in my own life is too,
and I can't afford to cry very often.

I'm glad I wept yesterday among friends.
I must find a way to gather these mountains
and carry them with me.

EarthRise at Winter's End

Let me withdraw from my kindred spirits here to rest
under a lonely oak here at the tag end of February.
Were it not for the stringy light green lace lichen,
this oak's hibernating branches would be barren.
People call it Spanish moss, but it's lace lichen.

The lichen is intriguing, but I want to concentrate
on this tree and similar oaks in grassy knolls
up and down California, and to include the oaks
in the Southern states, draped with genuine Spanish
moss, the oaks along the west coast of the Americas,

and all similar trees on earth. I want to embrace
all the world's oaks and their forebearers, including
the oak trees cited, twenty times, in the Bible. As I rest
peacefully under this oak at EarthRise, where lichens,
resembling necklaces strewn about after an explosively

enchanting evening, grow chaotically this time of year.
I'm truly blessed, surrounded by people who help me
understand what I need to cultivate and enjoy my harvest.
In winter's shadow I breathe in deeply and slowly release.
At this jeweled oak, I draw another breath, pause, and let go.

Shaking

Seconds ticked on—two, five—
offices no longer safe,
my windows bowing like plastic—ten—,
I needed shelter—fifteen,
spotted a desk across the hall,

I dove underneath, someone already there,
a large woman filling the entire space;
my head by her bottom—twenty,
sprinklerheads falling from the ceiling,
when it ended—twenty-three—we giggled.

Later, my little family unhurt,
our house undamaged, just power out.
We put our candles away and
headed for my parents' small apartment.

Perhaps I knew then, watching my mother,
her relaxed self after cocktails,
and my dad, temporary patriarch.
Perhaps I knew he would die, soon,
with as little warning as an earthquake.

He found this brand new two-foot flashlight
and together we inserted batteries.
I enjoyed a wonderful well-fathered moment
as it shone its first light
in this emergency explicable to anyone.

But soon the aftershocks started,
damned things, more earthquakes really, and reports
of how close we'd come to complete c\h/a\o/s,
people needing new foundations under old houses,
and new shaking, day or night.

Whatever we were doing, we'd run to the children,
hold them, then, quick, turn on TV.
Where's the epi-center? What's the Richter reading?

The next week a friend called saying children from
alcoholic families were particularly hard hit.
I said not me—I'm o\k/a\y.

How It Went

Friday Evening

> You are not with me,
> again.
> I call the kids and don't ask to speak to you—
> that is what you want, I think.

Friday Night

> You are not with me.
> With new friends, I sing songs in a meadow
> we watch for meteor showers.
> I almost call back, for you.

Saturday Morning

> You are not with me.
> Horses pass by in an elaborate city-to-city race.
> To finish, they have to climb that slope we stayed by.
> You are still sleeping, I'm sure.

The Soothing Touch of a Currycomb

Cats, horses and dogs know us in
many ways. When we address them
by name, they sometimes seem startled
at our voice, or even thrilled.

They know other words too, stay
and stop and come, and horses know
the secret language of tongue-clucks.
They know who feeds them and

bathes them, and who gives them a
treat, another word they know.
I've never known an animal who
doesn't like to be gently scratched

behind the ears or rubbed down.
Or patiently groomed with
A hard-bristled currycomb.
What they know about us for certain,
they know through touch.

Distractible

A new mare on the ranch.
The stallions wonder
What would that be like?
A top horsewoman
Told me she'd rather
Work with mares.
They're simpler.
They just go out
And do their jobs.

Carol Arnold on horseback.
Arnold Family collection.

Longing

Stop me if you've
heard enough longing,

watched me shiver,
wanting wild rivers.

I know you're downstream,
strong enough to pull me out.

God I miss you
on this safe shore.

Night on the Town. Carol and Kevin Arnold.
Arnold Family collection.

Feeding Other People's Horses

Even after ten years, Snowball, the male
pony, and Crystal, the thirty-year-old
thoroughbred, approach me, stamp a foot
and whinny in anticipation of carrots

and cookies. Of course I pet them. They're
all that's left of my horseback-riding days.
They mean so much, giving me my daily dose
of horse therapy, every day, thirty-five

hundred days of the eight-minute ride to
the hills to see them, not four or five days
a week—every day. When I take vacation,
I provide treats for volunteers who fill in.

People question whether I visit the horses
even when it rains and I ask back, Do you
think the rainy days are easy on them?
There's a small roof that tries to shelter

them, but some days the wind drives the rain
sideways. They shiver in their wet coats.
Those are not the days for me to skip feeding
and touching them, making me feel loved.

Carpaccio

Wine was already spilled on the pink tablecloth,
the two couples' cheeks already flushed,
but she hadn't noticed,
so when her husband split a shrimp cocktail with Bill's wife,
she surprised herself by joining with Bill to split Carpaccio.

The raw beef came laid out like a flower,
deep red petals on bone plate.

Bill spread capers and minced onions wantonly,
and didn't worry about seeds as he squeezed the lemon.

She could feel his hunger as he gathered the beef,
then, his fork still in his left hand,
took a large red chunk into his mouth;
from next to him she felt she could taste
onionpungent and lemonsour and capersalt—
despite herself she could taste them
merging on his tongue with the cool red flesh;

then in front of God and everybody in the nice restaurant,
in front of their shrimp-cocktail-eating spouses,
lifting her fork over the spilled wine,
she followed Bill's brazen lead.

Dancing at Halloween

All parts of love are here with us
as we ask one another to dance,
the women so festive in Halloween garb—
one tribal princess, several bats, a slinky disco woman,
and of course plump pumpkins, perky cowgirls.

Filial love abounds as we all smile too much,
chit-chatting about each other's children
and the price of real estate in the valley we overlook.

Erotic love taps our shoulders as the singer croons.
A few men still pose as predators, but most are cautious now,
single at midlife, and the women, comfortable
in their lonely bodies, know what they have to share.

Agape love is here too,
forgiving errant dance steps and premature marriages,
blessing the few souls not dancing now and even
those like me, making outdated movements
on the dance floor with one of the pumpkins.
I want to tell her that my new love, far away tonight,
is here with us too. The music slows and the singer,
portable mike in hand, walks onto the dance floor
and serenades us: it is time to go home.

Daylight Savings Time

It's one of those many things
I'd chosen to never worry about

but now that my son Scotty
has his own home, he wants

that precious hour after work
to overlook the Hudson Valley

from what was previously
a summer cabin and which

he's now sharing with either
a squirrel or a raccoon

who steals bits of food.
In that extra hour of daylight

Scotty puts out a safe trap,
so now I'm a fan of this national

ritual that was put in place to save
energy or our glorious country

from something awful
I forget just what.

The Art Opening

Our daughter Johnna has won three photography awards,
so my ex-wife and I treat her and her artist friends
to a restaurant dinner after an opening in San Francisco.
We sit one person apart, my ex-wife's husband
on the other side of her, subdued in a tie and tweed jacket.
Johnna sits between us, while little conversation bits filled
with double meanings flit around her, like
despite our differences we have done one thing well.

And my hurt foot, my bruised heel, fallen arch doesn't bother at all.
Johnna, often shy, seems oblivious to her aging mother and father
tonight, she is radiant in her moment, she has survived,
two of the show's sponsors will buy her oversized
black-and-white triptychs, so unexpectedly bold,
for more money than she spends in a month.
I bask in her reflected glory until, just as dessert arrives,
we're reminded the parking lot is closing, so I have to
ransom the car, and I can't get my loafers back on.

Why did I wear new shoes with this foot?
Johnna, suddenly solicitous, walks with me, supporting my arm.
The cold San Francisco winds have come, and every step hurts.
My ex- and her husband in his tweeds walk smoothly ahead.
I hobble and realize I am celebrating my daughter's success before
mine ever happened. I picture an airport, me gunning my plane—
there's not enough runway for me to get airborne. I shiver in my
shirtsleeves as I lean almost all my weight on Johnna now.

Chuck Close in the New Haven Museum

Chuck Close has two self-portraits,
one, black ink on white paper, the
other white on black, both use

identical-sized pixels, about one quarter
inch squares, so that there's a logical
reciprocity, where thirty percent gray tone

translates into seventy percent
white ink on black paper at sixteen
squares per inch. Technical brilliance.

I feel I know Chuck from seeing his work
in other museums—wonderful, but
the man manages to hide in plain sight.

Come forth, show us who you are,
come out from behind your pixilation—
all these are representations of *you*,

Charles Thomas Close, born in Monroe,
Washington, graduate of Yale,
undergrad and grad. *Just be Chuck.*

How She Left Him

He so loved the natural world that he
joined others who had come to art late
in life to patiently paint nature *al fresco*.

When his wife started having memory
problems, he tried to take it in stride.
She would be fine while he painted.

But things progressed and he spent more
time on doctor's visits and panic attacks,
pills and paperwork, every aspect of her life.

For the last years of her life, the *plein air*
artist stayed inside with her. When he
rejoined his friends in the open air,

he tried to explain how he'd lived for the
few moments she seemed her old self,
and how she left him before she left him.

Oleanders

If you get the urge to learn more about nature, don't tamp
it down. Do a little at a time. Oleanders are a good place to start.
They may not be flower shop pretty, but have their own charms.

Oleanders are shrubs but can grow almost as large as trees.
They come in white, pink, and red, with the white variety
being most prevalent, possibly because they're the hardiest.

Once you're tuned in, you'll see oleanders everywhere,
even along freeways, because they require little care.
And, given a warm climate, they can flower all year long.

But the real reason you might want to start studying flora
with oleanders came to me as a complete surprise—all
parts of the plant, even their roots, are extremely poisonous.

A few leaves in a pet's water dish can kill him. Janet Fitch named
her novel *White Oleander* because a girl is abandoned into
foster care when her mother uses the flower to kill her lover.

Once you've discovered oleanders, expand your knowledge
one plant at a time. You might jump next to hydrangeas, whose
flowers can appear as big as a salad plate of almost solid color,

not just white, pink, and red, but, with the right soil acidity, blue
or even purple. Colors so dense they're ready for the flower shop.
After oleanders and hydrangeas, other flowers will open up to you.

California Waste Land

We've passed that lion/lamb one,
Our bold flowers bloom again.
Long drought months have begun
A third of the year with no rain.

Now new troubles come to light
Alarming from Oregon to Mexico.
We watch our forests self-ignite
Our parched reservoirs so low.

Invitation

Sometimes I'm lost in gnarly oaks,
but tonight I find myself wandering
amidst hundreds of ruler-straight
redwood trees. I'm in my fantasy world,
complete with unicorns and pegacorns
and amiable women without agendas,
in California's wildflower-laden rolling hills.

I find an old growth redwood that has died,
perhaps felled, now surrounded by a ten-foot
circle of young trees people call a Fairy Circle
or a Cathedral. I build a bed of fronds at its
center, and throw down a blanket. Lying on
my back, I gaze up to the stars, and think
how perfect this would be with a lover.

Autumn Sun

Hints of moisture interrupt
the deep blue of the sky,
blend into just slightly lighter
blue where the cloud starts
and then the purest light blue,
growing fully white
and finally, a touch of gray,
and here, near sunset,
oh, that orange at the cloud's
edge, reflecting the autumn
sun, almost gone now.

Jasper Ridge Biological Preserve, Stanford.

Photograph by Anthony D. Barnosky, Director,
Jasper Ridge Biological Preserve, Stanford.

Used with permission.

First, Do No Harm

No matter how you work
to avoid it, there's no way
around a critical opening.
Even if you have little
confidence you'll finish
successfully, you must make
that first incision. Start
forcefully with the sharpest
instrument in your kitbag.

It's the same for a tumor
on the brain or a deep ache
in the reader's heart.
Poetry and surgery
are ancient brothers
like Romulus and Remus.

Minimize any bleeding
as you excise whatever
you know doesn't belong.
Once mended, close things up
with uniform cross-stitches
X X X X X X X X X X X X.
If you've operated with your
full attention and decisive care,
that last line begins the healing.

Poet Snow

Artists give us light—
it bends around corners
with all the variations of color

Musicians give us sound—
the whirr of a hummingbird's wing
the drumbeat of a needy child

Writers give us weather—
the heat in Atlanta
during the War Between the States.

Poets offer verse falling gently
to earth, blanketing mountains,
valleys and cities equally—like snow.

Angel's Emendations

Someone, or something,
has hacked into my computer
and made changes,

deleting extra words and
repeated phrases, sometimes
adding attributions.

The emendations all say
—"Changed at 3 AM by Angel"—
not a minute earlier or later.

She highlighted the three asterisks
* * * at the end with the comment,
"Getting close."

Mabel Arnold, Kevin Arnold, and Clara Arnold.

Photograph by Dr. Kate Arnold.

We Writers

I find a thunderstorm and hold
An umbrella high on a treeless
Golf course, hoping to experience
That lightning we all dream of.

Heart Grown Up

"It is better for the heart to break,
than not to break." —*Mary Oliver*

Until she broke you, I wasn't sure you
existed. At most, I thought of you
as just another organ—a gallbladder,

a spleen, or a liver. She ensured I felt
heartache not as tired metaphor but
as physical pain. She let you show me joy,

but also watched you radiating agony.
Ahead of me as usual, she introduced
me to my grown-up broken heart.

At Dawn How Close We Are to Death

In sleepy fog I knit dreams
on two busy needles:
daily routines and
fantasies of breaking out.

Then the fuzzy clarity of the last dark:
I vow to be easier on myself yet
work harder for the things I care about—
for a moment life seems simple and clear.

At daybreak I wander out:
a blanket-wrapped man
pushing a shopping cart
avoids my eye, then looks up.

We who are awake,
equal in that new light,
regard each other
as in a holy place.

At Jasper Ridge Ranch

She's teaching me about horses,
how you hang their halters
next to the stalls in case of fire,
and English saddles—almost bareback—
are not just *frou frou* but give the horse
the freedom to jump.
She says rhythmically moving
up and down on a horse
is like making love to a woman.
Perhaps, I think, a woman
you're not in love with,
but I am not yet a horseman.

The Chinese Woman's Voice

I get a few whiffs of foreign sawdust
while I fondle an imitation Ming vase,
nearly opaque with blue splotches,
hurriedly hand-painted
and a lid that doesn't quite seat
at an import store surrounded by
mugs stacked over my head
and dangling tables and baskets.

The sweet-pungent smell drags me not to
fifteenth-century China but
some quick-fingered assembly line painter.
I feel I can see her now
working furiously at her task.
I probably have things she covets:
money and time to spend with my kids
in a discount East-West shop.
She talks to me says
it's okay, it's okay.

Dad's Knights

I didn't choose a good year to beat you at chess,
didn't know what trouble you were in,
you with those slashing knights,
but who paid little attention to the openings,
never accepted that unless you open up the queen's side
she'll never sweep across that long diagonal and
change every relationship on the board.

Now your hopeful yellow alligator shirt hangs in my closet.
I wish I'd argued with you that year,
pointed my young finger to chess books that said
you have to develop the other pieces—
knights can't do it alone.

To the Guy Who Loved to Call Me Cuz

My mother's brother, Gerald Ayres's father,
Found his son's exuberance an awkward bother.

Still—sagacious, he was impossible to suppress—
Bounding from Yale to Hollywood with success.

Assistant to the head of Columbia Studios at twenty-eight,
Married to warm Annie. Father of two. Assumably straight.

Much younger, I had no idea what it meant to be gay then—
When he left his young family, I just couldn't forgive him.

As my life winds down past September,
The random scenes I somehow remember—

Chatting with Gerry about Oscar Wilde on a drive—
Why couldn't I stay closer while he was alive?

Left to Right: Randy Quaid, Jack Nicholson, Gerald Ayres.

Easter

I'm a Christian again this year.
The vote was close in my senate,
fifty to forty-seven, and was so
contentious in my house it never
got out of committee, so my old
designation held.

At church on Good Friday
they said when you dropped
your cross you performed no
miracles but lifted your
burden onto your shoulder
as all of us have to do.

Now Easter, the unexpected
empty tomb. I need your
forgiveness and resurrection.
If I can just quiet my legislature
for once, let love guide my life.
Let love lead me home.

Our True Song

Our simple acts may be the warp and weft
of the substance of our lives, what is left

beyond the gifts and wills, the trusts and estates
after our *belles lettres* or *plein air* landscapes

what if our day-to-day relationships, in the long
slog of life, form our lasting legacy, our true song?

Driven by Love

Perhaps one love is like another when it ends—
  only the one who wanted it to last
  understands the enormity of what's been lost.

At least once you must have lived in that lovesick daze
  and glanced up to see someone who looked
  almost exactly like the lover who scorned you,

and didn't you jump up from your table just to make sure,
  and run full-tilt wherever that person took you,
  driven by adrenaline, driven by hope?

And when, panting, you overtook this stranger,
  what did you do then? Were you apologetic,
  did you say, "Sorry, I mistook you..."

or did you find the righteous power of the jilted lover
  and set things straight right then and there,
  describing the monstrous treatment you'd received,

you, who could have made it all work! Did you seize the moment
  and tell the tale in that fervent, yet out-of-control,
  desperate way that we only get to perform a few times

in real life, standing squarely at center stage for once,
  stating, of all the people on this planet,
  you are one of the handful driven by love?

Acknowledgements

Thankful acknowledgement is made to the editors of the following journals and anthologies in which some of these poems appeared earlier:

Boston Phoenix Literary Review—"Arriving Late in a Marriage"

Cæsura, 25ᵗʰ Anniversary Issue—"Japanese Graveyard on Kauai"

Dallas Opera News—"Invitation to the Opera"

eNVee—"Carpaccio," as "Seeds"

Foothill Review—"Summer's Last Swim Meet" as "Free, Fly, Back, Breast"

Manzanita: Poetry and Prose of the Motherlode and Sierra, Vol. 5—"At Jasper Ridge Ranch" as "At Webb Ranch"

Mokhillian Review of Poetry—"Dancing at Halloween"

Mudfish Magazine—"Across the Decades," "Carpaccio," and "The Milkshake Guy"

Poems to Lift You Up & Make You Smile (Forthcoming anthology edited by Jayne Jaudon Ferrar) —"Our True Song"

Remembering—"Aerobatics in a Time of War"

Slippery Elm—"The Chinese Woman's Voice"

The Clock, Desperados, and Jeremy, the first Zapizdat Review—"Like Air," as "Maverick," "Dad's Knights" as "My Father on Horseback," and "Returning"

The Squaw Review—"How it Went"

Wine, Cheese & Chocolate, Manzanita Writers Press—"Carpaccio"

Online poetry websites:

YourDailyPoem.com, Jayne Jaudon Ferrar, editor:
March 1, 2011, "Invitation to the Opera"
August 19, 2011, "Summer's Last Swim Meet" as "Free, Fly, Back, Breast"
June 6, 2013, "American Shakespeare"
December 31, 2018, "Our True Song"
March 3, 2020, "Daylight Savings Time"
April 23, 2020, "The Colors of Jasper Ridge"

USRepresented.com, Eric Stephenson, editor, All part of Kevin's Much-loved Poems:
"Coming Home Late in a Marriage"
"One of a Handful," as "Driven by Love"
"Hooky from High School," as "Hooky"
"Invitation to the Opera"
"American Shakespeare"
"The Soothing Touch of a Currycomb" (as "Currycomb")

Five South Literary Review: "The Move to Memory Care" (forthcoming)

A grateful poet gives thanks . . .

Decades ago, when I was attending the Squaw Valley Community of Writers as a short story writer, *Robert Hass* enticed me by saying, "In Poland they say nothing happens until a poet writes about it." I vowed to return to the conference as a poet, which required . . . well, poems. I took a class from *Denise Levertov* at Stanford, and one from *Al Young*, who helped me publish my first poem. *Sharon Olds* invited me to join what had become a prestigious poetry week at Squaw Valley. As a nascent poet-duckling, I imprinted on *Galway Kinnell, Brenda Hillman, Sharon,* and *Robert*, who shaped my ideas of what poems could be. Galway, a marvel, told us, "Pretend you've met someone from another planet and want to show them what it's like to live on Earth." *Jane Hirshfield* gave me the title of my first novel, *Sureness of Horses,* edited by *Monika Rose and Suzanne Murphy,* and published by *Manzanita Writers Press.*

Somehow, I became President of the San Jose Center for Poetry and Literature, which we renamed Poetry Center San Jose, a group I led for thirteen years. There I met *Kathie Isaac-Luke*. Without Kathie, this collection wouldn't exist. She worked closely with Monika Rose to compile and edit this collection. At PCSJ, I also learned from so many, including *Nils Peterson, Sally Ashton, Mary Lou Taylor,* and *Erica Goss.*

I'm thankful to *Jill Hoffman,* who published my work early on in *Mudfish,* and her workshop, as well as *Jayne Jaudon Ferrer,* editor of *YourDailyPoem.com* and *Eric Stephenson,* editor of *USRepresented,* who published *Kevin's Most-loved Poems.* I'd be remiss not to thank *Brett Hall, Louis B. Jones,* and *Sands Hall* for continuing to lead the *Squaw Valley Community of Writers*—what a classy organization— and all the folks at *Waverley Writers,* including *Mary-Marsha Casoly, Joel Katz,* and *Steve Arntson.* And the founder of *Gold Rush Writers, Antionette May.* Thanks also to all countless others, who I've somehow overlooked.

Photograph by John Scott Caldwell Arnold.

About the Poet

Kevin is a transplanted Midwesterner who has lived in Palo Alto, California, most of his life. He has published in fifty literary magazines and has published a book of poems and a novel. The San Francisco/ Peninsula California Writer's Club recently named him Writer of the Year.

He served as President, Poetry Center San Jose, for twelve years, while he earned an MFA from San Jose State University. His novel, *The Sureness of Horses,* is available from Manzanita Writers Press in hardback, softcover, and ebook, and as an audiobook read by Sands Hall from Cherry Hill Publications.

His poems, praised for their accessibility, have been published widely. The national website *YourDailyPoem.com* has selected his poems eight times and has anthologized his work in their "Best of Your Daily Poem" collection *Poems to Lift You Up & Make You Smile.*